Revised Edition

STEVE & WENDY BACKLUND

IGNITING *Faith*
IN 40 DAYS

THE POWER OF HOPE, DECLARATIONS AND NEGATIVITY FASTS

© copyright 2012 Steve & Wendy Backlund, Igniting Hope Ministries
www.ignitedhope.com

Cover Design : Linda Lee www.LindaLeeCreates.com
Interior Design and Formatting : Lorraine Box PropheticArt@sbcglobal.net

Many thanks to the following people for their input in the writing of these devotionals:
Elaine Smith, Dale Kaz, Jeanie Sandahl, Michelle Alderson, Maureen Puddle, Holly
Hayes, Jared Neusch, Bob Arnold, Kim McGan, Wendee Fiscus and David Weigel.

ISBN: 13 978-0-9854773-0-1

this book is dedicated to

our children
Joel, Kyle and Heidi
Thank you for the joy you have brought into our lives.
We are so proud of you.

the churches we have pastored in
Round Mountain, Nevada
&
Weaverville, California
Thank you for believing in us and loving us
in so many ways.

and two men who paved the way...
Bill Johnson & Kris Vallotton

Thank you for following your dream
and paying a price so we could find God
and His goodness in a way we never thought we could!

how to use this book.

*Igniting Faith in 40 Days** has two major components. The first is the daily devotional teaching, which will strengthen you through its biblical principles of faith. The second is the speaking forth of the declarations mentioned in steps two and three below - "faith comes by hearing" (Romans 10:17).

Even though there is benefit in just reading this book, consider this radical format to maximize its contents:

1. **Read** a teaching (devotional) each day for 40 days.

2. **Boldly speak** the declaration for the devotional.

3. **Boldly speak** one of the declaration lists from Appendix One (do *both morning and night*).

4. **Read** selected chapters form the books of Mark, Galatians, Proverbs, Romans, Philippians, and Hebrews during the 40 days. See Appendix Two for the Suggested Bible Reading Plan.

5. **Listen** to one or all of these CD series during the 40 days: *Relentless Mind Renewal*, *Victorious Faith*, or *Framing Our Future*. Available at www.ignitedhope.com

6. **Go** on a NEGATIVITY FAST (also called a POSITIVITY FEAST) during the 40 days. This book is an ideal resource to use during this kind of fast. Ideas for your negativity fast are available on page vi.

7. **Maximize your experience** by tracking your journey with the 40 day checklist on page viii.

8. **Finally**, and most importantly, find one or more others to join you in this experience.

*The message of this book is not a single formula of success, but a necessary ingredient to add to a life of intimacy with Jesus.

40 day negativity fast

What a Negativity Fast is *NOT*

1. It is not denying that problems exist.
2. It is not *stuffing things* that are wrong.
3. It is not critical of others who may be struggling.
4. It is not irresponsible concerning things that need to be done.

What a Negativity Fast *IS*

1. It is determining to focus more on God's promises than on problems.
2. It is learning to speak with hope about even the toughest of issues.
3. It is becoming *solution focused* rather than *problem focused*.
4. It is refraining from reacting and giving voice to pessimism, criticism of others, self-criticism and other forms of unbelief.
5. It is speaking about problems to the right people in the right way.
6. It is replacing negative words and thoughts with positive words and thoughts based on the promises of God.

Note: It is crucial to not only stop thinking and speaking unbelief and negativity, but to grow in thinking and speaking the positive – truth, the promises of God, praising God, encouragement to others and thanksgiving. *The negative must be replaced with the positive in order for this fast to be effective.*

Igniting Faith in 40 Days has been used by many as a daily devotional book to read during a personal or group 40 day negativity fast.

declarations of faith

"Faith comes by hearing..."
Romans 10:17

We want to help you in your faith journey. We have recorded all the declarations of this book on one mp3 so that you can hear and declare the promises of God with us.

To download this free *Declarations to Ignite Faith* mp3, visit us at www.ignitingfaithdownload.com and enter the following code:

SC477T3ER

tracking your journey

To further help you in your faith journey, we have developed this 40 day checklist and a Suggest Bible Reading Plan found in Appendix Two.

BR Bible Reading **RD** Read Devotional **DD** Spoke Devotional Declaration
OD Other Declarations from the back of book
NF Negativity Fast/Positivity Feast

Day	BR	RD	DD	OD	NF/PF
1					
2					
3					
4					
5					
6					
7					
8					
9					
10					
11					
12					
13					
14					
15					
16					
17					
18					

Day	BR	RD	DD	OD	NF/PF
19					
20					
21					
22					
23					
24					
25					
26					
27					
28					
29					
30					
31					
32					
33					
34					
35					
36					
37					
38					
39					
40					

contents

introduction

I invite you on a forty-day journey to change the way you think so that you can live the abundant life Jesus promised in John 10:10.

Freedom and *transformation* come from believing truth instead of lies (John 8:32). The quality of our lives and the advancement of God's Kingdom depend on "renewing the spirit of our minds" (Ephesians 4:22- 24; Romans 12:2).

Wendy and I have learned that *true faith is built on hope;* a confident, optimistic expectation that good is coming based on God's promises and a revelation of His goodness.

This book is filled with hope for you, your family, your church, your city, and your nation.

Get ready to grow. Get ready to declare God's promises. Get ready for transformation. Today is the first day of the rest of your life. We bless you as you *ignite your faith.*

Steve Backlund

LEGAL vs. EXPERIENTIAL OWNERSHIP

Every place... I have given you.
Joshua 1:3

oshua chapter one is the chapter for those ready to leave wilderness Christianity. Joshua was called to lead the new generation into the Promised Land. In verse two, God says, "Go... to the land which I am giving to them." He adds in verse three, "Every place that the sole of your foot will tread upon, I have given you." Then verse four gives the boundaries to what was theirs.

It's fascinating that they are told what is legally theirs before they experientially possess it. Legal ownership was no guarantee of experiential ownership. It was called the Promised Land so that they would confidently proceed to possess it – no matter what obstacles they encountered.

It is no different for us today. We have our own promised land. It's not a geographical area, but it is specific blessings and promises. For instance, every person has the legal ownership of eternal life, but that must be possessed experientially through faith in Christ. Also, God promises us health, favor, spiritual power, protection, abundant provision, wisdom, and much more. Peter refers to the "exceedingly great and precious promises" which were given to us "that we may be partakers of the divine nature" (2 Peter 1:4). We may have to overcome many challenges to experience these promises, but we can. Let's persevere and keep seeking to possess what is already legally ours.

Declare

I am who the Bible says I am.
I have what it says I have.
I can do what it says I can do.
I increasingly possess, in my experience, the promises of God.

A LYING APPLE TREE

Calling those things that are not...
Romans 4:17

*A*n apple tree will produce apples because of what it is. When it is young, it will have no apples; but it still must say, "I am an apple tree." When it is winter and there are no apples; it still says, "I am an apple tree." Is it lying at those times? No. It would be lying to say anything different.

Many Christians have a hard time saying who God says they are when no fruit is manifesting in that particular area. Could they be too young in that truth to be fruitful? Could they be in a season where that dimension of the Christian life is being pruned back for future growth? Either way, it does not mean they are lying when they say, "I am anointed, prosperous, delivered, healed, righteous, strong etc." Joel 3:10 says, "Let the weak say I am strong." We don't deny the fact of weakness, but we focus on the greater truth that we are strong in Him.

Again, because the Word says we ARE these things, we would be untruthful to say anything different. Let's not lie against the truth. Indeed, we ARE what the Bible says we are.

Declare

I am who the Word says I am. I have a sound mind.
I have great favor with God and man. People love me.
I am a happy person. I love life and enjoy every day.
I walk in divine health. I have abundant provision.
I am blessed and protected.
I increasingly know who and what I am in Christ.
I make a tremendous difference for Christ wherever I go.

BRINGING LIFE TO DEAD PLACES

Let the weak say "I am strong."
Joel 3:10

*G*od has called us to make dead things alive. In Ezekiel 37, the prophet was asked if the dry bones could live. In the dialogue and events that followed, God showed Ezekiel and His people a powerful principle that is vital for us today.

God's method of bringing life to these very dry bones was through Ezekiel prophesying "life" to the whole situation. Ezekiel had to speak to the bones. He had to prophesy to the wind. As he did, things changed and life came.

You and I also must continually speak to dead areas in our lives and circumstances. A main method of God bringing change to a situation is for one of His children to speak His promises over people and circumstances. "God, who gives life to the dead and calls those things which do not exist as though they did" (Romans 4:17).

It starts with each of us prophesying life over ourselves. Joel gives us a good place to start in Joel 3:10, "Let the weak say, 'I am strong.'" Start now a life long habit to call "those things which do not exist as though they did" in your life.

Declare

Even though I feel weak at times, I am really strong.
I am very strong to accomplish God's purposes in my life,
And to be a strength to others.
I prophesy daily over my circumstances, my future,
And over the dry areas of my life.

If you don't understand something written in this book, just set that aside and continue on your journey. Most things will be clarified in the 40 days.

PRAYING IN FAITH

Mary has chosen the best part.
Luke 10:42

Often people spend much effort and time praying over a circumstance hoping that time and quantity of prayer will bring the desired result. The hope is that perhaps faith will increase through this effort and thus the prayer will be answered.

This kind of thinking implies that faith is built by the amount of time and energy expended. We need to understand that faith does not come through our effort. Faith is a result of what we know. Our "measure of faith" (Romans 12:3) will increase in proportion to the revelation we have of God's character, His love, and His promises toward us.

Often we do not realize the value of spending time with God when we are not praying for needs. The reason we worship, quietly wait in His presence, and search the scripture is mainly to build a relationship and to learn about the character, power, and love of God. Our intimacy and relationship with Him will have a direct correlation to our level of faith; not because it earns us more authority, but because it gives something for our faith to stand on.

Declare

*My trust and faith in God grows in proportion to how much
I know His character, goodness, and trustworthiness.
I therefore spend much time in His presence
developing intimacy with Him.
Never become satisfied with a mere theology of
God's presence in your private life or church life.
Pursue His manifested presence!*

PRAYING IN FAITH

Prayer ...avails much
James 5:16

5

*A*s we battle spiritual forces, it is important to distinguish between the burden of the Lord and the weight of unbelief.

We must take inventory of our emotions as we pray. Is a spirit of fear, anxiety, or hopelessness present? Do we feel "under the circumstance" that we are praying about? Are we consistently begging for God's help? If so, the heaviness we are feeling is probably not about the circumstance we are facing, but from our own beliefs about God and life.

These emotions are not going to go away just by praying longer, fasting, or praying harder. We also cannot pretend these emotions are not there. We need to confront them and rebuke spirits of unbelief, fear, and hopelessness. We can start this by repenting of wrong core beliefs that hinder confidence in the power of our prayers. Then we must turn our eyes to God's faithfulness and worship Jesus until we get a revelation of His goodness and love toward us. The battle is first in us and then in our circumstances.

Declare

Fear and doubt are my main enemies.
I am not a victim to these emotions.
I replace the lies fueling them with the promises of God.
I trust in the goodness of God.

"Spirits of heaviness" in private or corporate prayer result from seeing the problem as bigger than God. Stir up God's promises before praying!

6 DEALING WITH UNCERTAINTY

Do not be anxious about anything.
Philippians 4:6

God's great promises empower us to "be partakers of the divine nature, having escaped the corruption that is in the world through lust" (2 Peter 1:4). What a statement about the power of promises!

Here are five promises to get into your spirit to "blast away" uncertainty about the future:

I Can - Philippians 4:13 says, "I can do all things through Christ who strengthens me." Whatever is needed from me, I can do it.

There is a Way - I Corinthians 10:13 reveals there is a way for every person (whether to get out of a tough time or to get into God's purpose).

I've Prayed - James 5:16,17 tells us that our prayers are powerful and effective. Things will be different because we pray.

God Will Finish What He Has Started - Philippians 1:6 tells us to be confident of God's finishing power.

It Will Be OK - Romans 8:28 says that all things will work for good in my life as I focus on two things: God's call for me, and loving Jesus Christ first in my life.

Declare

God's exceedingly great and precious promises
help me to wage war in my mind against lies about the future.
I therefore cannot be defeated in Jesus' name.
I am more than a conqueror.

CUT OFF FROM GRACE

... miracles ...by the hearing of faith?
Galatians 3:5

*H*e who supplies the Spirit to you and works miracles among you, does He do it by the works of the law, or by the hearing of faith?" (Galatians 3:5). This is probably the second most important question in the Bible. (Only "Who do you say that I [Jesus] am?" in Matthew 16:15 would be more important.) The Apostle Paul asks this penetrating question in the book of Galatians, which is a "must read" and "must study" for the advancing saint. He was rebuking those in Galatia for returning to a performance-based religion instead of keeping a faith-based relationship. It is a strong book with strong words such as, "You who attempt to be justified by the law; you have fallen from grace" (Galatians 5:4).

Grace is the empowerment to do God's will. Most people probably think that persistence in sin leads to a cutting off of the flow of grace; but, in reality, we are cut off from God's power when we believe that God is more concerned with our behavior than He is with our beliefs.

Here's a truth that will keep us in grace: What is believed about something is more important than what is done about it. Good works are important, but they primarily result from a proper belief system in our lives.

Declare

I reject a works-based Christianity.
I declare I have faith to receive all of God's blessings
and power to change my life and the world.
I now receive a new measure of grace through faith.

ROSE COLORED GLASSES

… through …Scriptures …might have hope.
Romans 15:4

$\mathcal{S}$ometimes optimistic people are accused of seeing life through "rose colored" glasses. Their vision supposedly is affected by an unrealistic perspective that blinds them to life's negatives and accentuates only the positives.

All Christians have predispositions that influence how the Bible is interpreted, and in turn, how life is viewed. These unconscious inclinations are often influenced by the "traditions of men" which limit positive expectancy for the future (see Mark 7:13).

Romans 15:4 tells us that hope results from proper Bible "learning." Later in verse 13 we are told that joy, peace, and abounding hope come from believing. There should be a corresponding increase of hope in our lives that is proportional to the amount of the Bible we consume.

Unfortunately, many church teachings limit hope. For example, most end times teachings decrease positive expectation for lives, families, cities, and the nations of the world. As a result, many don't live with hope and faith because of a predisposition that believes the world is getting worse (and not better). This hopelessness indicates we need an alteration in our interpretation of Scripture. Truly, hope grows with each encounter with God's Word and with the God of hope.

Declare

I see the Bible and life through "blood colored" glasses,
seeing through the finished work of the cross.
I therefore abound in hope for my life and for everyone connected to me.
God's promises are true.
My prayers are powerful and effective.
My hope helps release God's kingdom in our midst.

WHO DO YOU THINK YOU ARE?

… but your name shall be called Abraham.
Genesis 17:5

9

*A*bram received a promise that his descendents would be as numerous as the stars in the sky and the sand on the seashore. The problem was that he was very old, and his wife was past childbearing years and had been barren all of her life. The prophetic word concerning his innumerable descendants was laughable to the landlocked mind.

After more than two decades of no manifestation of the promise, it seemed even more impossible. Although Abram's faith grew, there was still no baby for Sarah and him.

Finally, at 100 years old, they had their promised son, Isaac (which means laughter). What made the difference? The key change was this: Abram's name was changed to Abraham (which means "father of a multitude"). As Abram called himself by the promises of God, "he was strengthened in faith" and saw the promise come to pass. (See Romans 4 for insight on this process.)

So who do you think you are? Is your identity shaped by your past or by the promises of God? Your answer will largely determine whether God's seemingly laughable promises over your life will come to pass.

Declare

> *I am who God says I am. I can do what He says I can do.*
> *I will see His promises come to pass in me as I speak*
> *His promises over my life.*

We won't have it because we say it,
but saying it is a big part of having it.

10 (PART II)
WHO DO YOU THINK YOU ARE?

Calling those things that are not, as though they were.
Romans 4:17

*H*ere is a major life question: Does our experience create our identity, or does our identity create our experience? The answer is... (drum roll please)... our identity creates our experience. Remember, those who think they can, and those who think they can't, are both right (consider the spies in Numbers 13 and 14). What we believe about ourselves will either bind us or launch us.

When it comes to who we think we are, God is calling us to believe His Word instead of negative experience. He says "Reckon yourselves to be dead indeed to sin, but alive to God..." (Romans 6:11), and "Let the weak say 'I am strong'" (Joel 3:10). Abraham "did not consider his own body, already dead..." (Romans 4:19).

Satan, on the other hand, wants us to focus on our failures and lack. A battle rages in our souls concerning what to believe about ourselves. Do we "call ourselves" by our negative experience or by God's promise. Proverbs 23:7 declares as a man "thinks in his heart, so is he." Let's think God's thoughts about us, and nothing less.

Declare

I am a new creation in Christ.
Old things have passed away.
All things are new.
I am strong in Christ.
I am who the Bible says I am.

NON-NEGOTIABLE CONVICTIONS

Daniel... three times a day... prayed...
as was his custom since his early days.
Daniel 6:10

11

*D*aniel was a man of conviction. Even the threat of the lion's den did not move him away from his godly habits. He built his life around life-producing priorities. In contrast, the prophet Malachi rebuked the people of his day for giving their leftovers to the Lord (see Malachi chapter one). Unlike Daniel, they began to view God as a burden rather than a delight.

Two things cause convictions that burn in our hearts which become non-negotiable: loving God's presence, and a strong vision for the future. Without these, we will only give God our leftovers.

Here are areas for your convictions to develop in: time with God and His Word, fellowship and worship, serving in ministry, financial giving, speaking God's promises, prioritizing our family, having strong accountability relationships, and putting ourselves in places where God's power can touch our lives and the lives of others.

Like Daniel, do you have spiritual non-negotiable convictions? Or are you fighting the "leftover battle" as the people in Malachi's day? Today is the first day of the rest of your life. Believe He will empower you to build your schedule around God's priorities like never before. You won't be sorry.

Declare

I give God the first portion of my life and He takes care of all my needs.
I am a person of conviction.
I have dominion over my life and my time.
I burn with a personal vision that leads me to
sacrifice for God and His presence.

12

DO NOT SAY...

Do not say I am only a youth.
Jeremiah 1:7

*H*as anyone ever told you, "Don't say that?" Probably. We've all been guilty of speaking something we shouldn't have. Well, Jeremiah experienced someone "calling him out" on what he said. That someone happened to be God. He challenged Jeremiah's self-restricting statement, "I am only a youth."

God had already told him, "Before I formed you in the womb... I ordained you a prophet to the nations." Jeremiah, however, focused on his apparent limitations rather than on the word of the Lord. He uttered an "I can't do that" proclamation that many in the church today would have applauded as true humility. God, however, said, "Do not say that."

Remember, those who say "I can" and those who say "I can't" are both right. Now is the time for us to take another look at what we speak; especially when we declare what we think we cannot do. Our words are either a rudder to direct our lives into God's prophetic will (James 3:5) or a curse that puts fences around our potential.

We must believe before we see (not the other way around). One of the main truths we are to believe is Philippians 4:13, "I can do all things through Christ..."

Declare

I renounce every curse I have spoken over my life
through declarations of what I thought I could not do.
I will not limit God, but will release Him by joining
Apostle Paul's positive declaration in saying "I CAN!"

WHERE AM I?

Out of the abundance of the heart the mouth speaks.
Matthew 12:33

13

*I*f you want to know where you are and where you are going in your spiritual life, listen to your own words. Jesus said, "Out of the abundance of the heart the mouth speaks. A good man out of the good treasure of his heart brings forth good things, and an evil man out of the evil treasure brings forth evil things" (Matthew 12:34-35). He then adds that, on the day of judgment, we will give an account for every "idle" word we speak (verse 36).

The word "treasure" in verse 35 could be translated "deposit;" thus, whatever has been deposited in our lives will come out in words. Our words are powerful forces that not only reveal our spiritual condition, but also dynamically impact our future and that of others.

Where are we? Our words are our indicator - especially words spoken when we are under pressure. Where are we going? Like a ship's rudder, our words will direct our destiny (James 3:4,5). What, then, do we need to do?

Radically make good deposits through thinking about and speaking God's truths. How do we know if we are ready for the next level in God? It's when our words consistently speak faith, hope, and love in the level we are in now.

Declare

My mouth is a powerful instrument for God's kingdom.
I daily make good deposits into my heart.
My words increasingly reveal a heart full of faith, full of hope, and full of love.

If we radically change our words about God and ourselves, we will find a shortcut through the wilderness of life.

14

KRATOS POWER

The word of God grew mightily & prevailed.
Acts 19:20

*T*here are three main Greek words for power in the New Testament. The first is *dunamis* - an explosive, "dynamite" power (Acts 1:8 – "but you shall receive power when the Holy Spirit has come upon you"). The second is *exousia* - a power based on authority (John 1:12 – KJV "But as many as received him, to them gave he power to become the sons of God"). *Dunamis* is the policeman's gun, while *exousia* is the badge. The third power word is *kratos* - a societal transforming power (Acts 19:20 – "the word of the Lord grew mightily and prevailed"). *Dunamis* and *exousia* manifest mostly in personal ministry, meetings, and intercessory prayer, while *Kratos* is an inner attitude of faith that holds a family, church, region, or nation in increasing blessings (the word "grew").

Elijah walked in *kratos* power when his prayer caused a three-year drought. This happened because he practiced a powerful prayer truth: what is believed after prayer is just as important as what is believed during prayer. Elijah's *kratos* faith continued after the prayer meeting. Romans 16:20 says, "The God of peace will crush Satan under your feet shortly." As we mix God's word with faith, we will experience growing inner peace. This increasing peace lets us know that the manifestation of Satan's "crushing" is drawing near. Philippians 4:6,7 also speaks to this. We are commanded not to worry about anything, but to pray about everything with THANKSGIVING. It's this on-going thanksgiving that helps produce a *kratos* power - the inner attitude of faith that holds us in increasing blessing. When we water yesterday's prayers with thanksgiving today, we build up an "Elijah" kind of prayer that avails much.

Declare

I radically thank God for the prayers I prayed yesterday.
I am thus growing in peace and kratos power that helps hold my life
and others in the increasing blessing of God.

NEVER ENOUGH

...works ...or the hearing of faith.
Galatians 3:2, 5

15

*T*he devil wants us to believe that we are not doing enough to see revival happen. "If you do a little more," he says, "then it will really happen." He wants us to think that we are constantly falling short. He tempts us to focus more on doing than on believing.

"There isn't enough unity for revival."

"People aren't praying enough."

"You should have fasted one more day."

"You haven't gone long enough without sinning in that area."

We must resist the temptation to think that these fruits of revival are the cause of revival. If we don't, we will believe we are not ready or deserving of a continual outpouring. This negative belief can actually be a main blockage to our revival experience.

Again, many say, "Breakthrough and revival are 'just around the corner.' We're close, but..." Someone must respond to this by saying, "No! Revival began on the day of Pentecost in Acts 2. It's not about working more for it; it's about believing that Jesus has already done everything that we could never do. He's done enough! Let us, by faith, release the manifestation of revival now!"

Declare

I am walking in personal revival.
It's already here, and I have chosen to believe it.
I have received this outpouring from God by faith, not by works.
As I believe, I am propelled to pray, to live in unity, to live in personal
obedience, and to live sacrificially for kingdom advancement.

END TIMES THEOLOGY

The gospel of the kingdom...
Matthew 24:14

*W*hat do you believe about the end times? Will there be revival or will the world "go to hell in a hand basket" before Jesus returns? Will the church limp into heaven or will she have "made herself ready" and become the bride "without spot or wrinkle?" Our answers are crucial.

Matthew 24:14 says that the "gospel of the kingdom will be preached in all the world" before the end. Scripturally, the kingdom gospel demonstrates power with signs and wonders following. That does not sound like a weak church in the last hour.

One obstacle to having a victorious end time mindset is that many theologians seem to place most of the Bible's positive last days' promises in the millennium. End times books reinforce this mindset; thus, our responsibility and expectation for kingdom advancement is diminished.

Consider this question: If a prophecy of judgment is given against a certain place, should Christians run to or run from that place? Biblical promises and commands would say, "Go and be salt. Preserve this place. Your presence will withhold devastation, save the people and make the difference." Why don't we think this way more? Could it be that we believe incorrectly about the end times?

Declare

The church is triumphant.
The end time church will be a "revival church"
full of power and Christ-likeness.

REMEMBER YOUR BENEFITS

Forget not all His benefits.
Psalms 103:2

*I*magine an employee with a generous benefit package. What would you think if he paid for all his medical bills, but had health insurance? He would be either ignorant or foolish. Unfortunately, we as the people of God, often do this by being ignorant of the fantastic benefits of being a child of God.

The Psalmist says, "Bless the Lord, oh my soul, and forget not all His benefits: Who forgives all your iniquities, Who heals all your diseases..." (Psalms 103:2,3). We are instructed to deliberately remember what is in our salvation package. The obvious implication is this: If we don't remember, we will believe we have to pay for things that have already been given to us.

We can't forget what we have never known. Some Christians are unaware that healing and other benefits are part of our salvation package. The Greek word *sozo* is translated "to save" in the New Testament; but it also means "to heal," "to deliver," and "to be made whole." It is refreshing that now there is a growing understanding that healing and transforming forgiveness are still benefits for the Christian, and are not just occasional sovereign blessings.

"Not forgetting" is more than a one time event. It is a lifelong contending for God's total benefit package for mankind. Truly, let's tell our soul to bless God and to radically remember how good He really is.

Declare

God is continually revealing to me my benefits as a Christian.
I contend for these in my soul;
thus, I experience them more and more in my life.

18 PRESUMPTUOUS FAITH

Abraham... was strengthened in faith.
Romans 4:20

*P*resumptuous faith is based more on feelings than on God's promises. There are two common areas where presumptuous faith occurs. The first is when we make faith decisions primarily through someone else's revelation (e.g. refusing medical treatment "by faith" because of another's testimony). The second can happen when we believe for a very specific, personal blessing (e.g. receiving that promotion, marrying so & so, having God providing for or vindicating us in that way, etc.).

Presumptuous faith can be avoided by remembering these three important things:

Build hope before "claiming" something specific by faith – Hope is the confident expectation that good is coming. It is an overall optimistic attitude concerning the future. A positive stronghold of hope decreases the likelihood that we will believe that God can only meet our need in one way.

Strengthen faith by believing for small things – Presumptuous people want to express a $1,000,000 faith when they have not even used their faith on the $100 level.

Walk with others concerning faith – Stay away from cynics and doubters, but find people who can help you discern presumption from real faith. Also, trust God to use spiritual mentors in clarifying His will and His voice.

Declare

I am strengthened in faith daily.
My belief system is built on a solid foundation of hope.
I am protected from presumptuous faith by hope, wisdom, and powerful people in my life.

Repent, for the kingdom of heaven is at hand.
Matthew 4:17

A good definition of repentance is to *change the mind.* The prefix *re-* means *again, anew, back or backward. Pent* is the highest place - as in *penthouse.* Repentance therefore could be defined as *going back to the highest place of thinking.*

Repentance is more than feeling sorry for the wrong things we have done. It is much more than seeking forgiveness and purposing to not sin again. It is important to repent to something, not just from something. It involves changing the mind from one course into a higher course.

We can cry our eyes out and not repent. True repentance is a decision to bring "every thought into captivity to the obedience of Christ" (2 Corinthians 10:5). It's not just a defensive reaction, but it is an offensive plan that moves God's kingdom from "being at hand" to becoming our experience.

The kingdom of heaven is God's abundant life of salvation, peace, power, evangelism, integrity, purity, miracles, strong families, health, prosperity, blessings and more. We are commanded to pray "Your kingdom come. Your will be done on earth as it is in heaven" (Matthew 6:10). This is God's highest place for His people. Our repenting creates an expectation that these will manifest; and this faith pulls them into our experience and into the experience of others. Praise God! Let's take our repenting to a new level today.

Declare

I capture my thoughts and take them to God's highest place.
I repent TO my promised land and
not just FROM my past negative behavior.
I keep repenting daily by joyfully speaking God's promises over my life.

SAINTS OR SINNERS

Paul... to the saints in Ephesus.
Ephesians 1:1

*A*s Christians, are we saints or sinners? The answer is crucial. If we misdiagnose ourselves and other Christians, it will have dire consequences.

The Bible says that we are saints. Our conversion changed our identity. Some would say that this is only a matter of words. It is not. What we call ourselves is vital to walking in God's fullness.

A main reason Christians continue sinning is because they believe that it is their nature to sin. Instead, we are to believe we are dead to sin and alive to God who will cause us to make good choices (Romans 6:11-13). As we do, we will see obedience grow in our lives. Our experience will always catch up to what we truly believe.

Christian leaders also need to see their *flocks* as saints. If we believe we are leading sinners, then control and fear will dominate our leadership. If the people are seen as saints, then empowerment and positive expectation will reign (which will bring out the best in those being led).

As always, the true test in this comes when there is a failure. Do we allow the failure to strengthen the negative stronghold of *sinnerhood*; or do we challenge it and say, "There may have been sin, but that is not our true identity"?

Declare

I am a saint.
I am prone to doing things right.
I see other Christians as saints also.
I will see increased obedience in my life
and in the lives of those I influence.

SOMETHING GREATER THAN CHARACTER

Now hope does not disappoint.
Romans 5:5

Romans 5:3-4 gives a tremendous road map for breakthrough. "We also glory in our tribulations, knowing that tribulation produces perseverance; and perseverance, character; and character, hope." Character would seem to be a final goal for the Christian, but there is something beyond character that must be possessed; it's hope.

Hope is the confident expectation of good coming. It is an overall optimistic attitude about the future based on the goodness and promises of God. Hope joins faith and love as the "big three" of Christianity (I Corinthians 13:13). Romans 15:13 says, "Now may the God of hope fill you with all joy and peace in believing, that you may abound in hope by the power of the Holy Spirit." Abounding hope is our goal.

Biblical hope is radical optimism for us, others, our family, the church, our communities, and beyond. This positive expectation releases God's promises in a way that character never could (for kingdom life does not manifest because of good works but by our faith). Godly character cannot be bypassed, but there is something more that is truly needed (hope) to impact the world in exponential ways.

Declare

My future is as bright as the promises of God.
I therefore am a person of abounding hope.
I expect God's goodness to increase daily
in my life and surroundings.

22 THE CRUCIAL MOMENT

Taking every thought captive.
2 Corinthians 10:5

*W*hat are the most important moments in the life of a growing Christian? Is it a powerful God encounter? Is it a fresh dedication to the purposes of God? Is it when we hear what the Spirit is saying to the church?

While these are important, I propose that there is another "God moment" that will have a greater effect on our destiny than these. What is it? It's when we fail or have experiences that do not line up with the promises of God.

In that moment, we have a choice. Do we keep our identity (and God's identity) in His promises, or do we use experience to empower a negative identity for us and for God? We must remember that negative strongholds are created and strengthened when we put our experiences above God's Word.

When failure happens, we must think like this: "I may have sinned, but I am not a sinner. I may have had an accident, but I have a covenant of protection. I may be in lack, but I am a prosperous person. Healing may not have manifested, but I am healed and bring healing to others." I don't deny my experience, I just don't create my identify from it. I may need help from others concerning the failure, but I resist the temptation to make negative conclusions from it.

Those who passively rely on experience to identify who they are (and who God is) will greatly limit God in their lives; however, those who seize these crucial moments by taking thoughts captive will powerfully break down restrictive strongholds and enter into their promised land.

Declare

I rejoice in apparent times of failure.
These are my crucial moments in life.
I am who the Bible says I am.

23

Your faith has made you well.
Mark 5:34

*T*he book of Mark reveals the power of faith in the individual's life. Here are some great examples of this:

"When Jesus saw **their faith**, He (forgave and healed)." Mark 2:5

"Daughter, **your faith** has made you well." Mark 5:34

"If you can believe, all things are possible to **him who believes**." Mark 9:23

"Go your way, **your faith** has made you well." Mark 10:52

"Have faith in God... whoever says to this mountain, 'be removed'... and does not doubt... but **believes**... he will have whatever he says... whatever things you ask when you pray, believe that you receive them, and you will have them." Mark 11:22-24

God's full salvation is released by faith. It is also restricted by unbelief (*see* Mark 6 where Jesus was limited by a lack of faith in Nazareth, and look also at Mark 4:40; 9:19).

A major turning point in the Christian life is this: having the belief that our faith makes a difference in what we and our descendants experience in health, prosperity, mental clarity, ministry effectiveness, longevity of life, blessings, and protection; and believing that our unbelief will restrict the flow of these kingdom benefits. Surely these thoughts must be understood in cooperation with other important truths; but we must believe our faith (or our unbelief) makes a difference, or we will live far below God's highest will for our lives.

Declare

Like Abraham, I am strengthened in faith daily.
Kingdom advancement and kingdom benefits are increasingly being
released in my life because of my faith. I am a difference maker for
everyone in my life; both now and after I leave planet earth.

24 WALKING OFF A SPIRITUAL ROOF

Meditate on... the law day and night.
Joshua 1:8

*C*an you imagine someone walking off a two-story roof, breaking his leg and then blaming God for what happened? That would be ridiculous. Well, that is in essence what some do by ignoring the laws of the spirit.

A law is "a scientific fact or phenomenon that is unchanged under given conditions" (Encarta World English Dictionary). The law of gravity is an example of this. Gravity needs to be understood and allowed to control every day decisions or there could be serious consequences!

It is also foolish to not live by spiritual laws – which are just as real and also must be grasped and applied. Scripture speaks of these laws, or spiritual principles, that ultimately control the natural dimension that we live in. It is important that we understand that there are truths to be esteemed for safe and successful living (whether it is the law of honor, honesty, sexual purity, agreement, sowing and reaping, tithing, faith, or speaking life). We are ignorant if we think that our choices, thoughts, and words have no consequences.

So, are you walking off a two-story roof in the spirit realm, thinking you can defy the laws of the spirit? It won't work. You'll get hurt. Cry out now for the heavenly wisdom to know what is real and true. You'll be blessed.

Declare

I love God's laws.
They are revealed to me daily.
Through Jesus, I walk in the laws of God.

WALKING OFF A SPIRITUAL ROOF

Meditate on... the law day and night.
Joshua 1:8

*T*he law of gravity can either work for us or against us. Stepping off a cliff will cause pain, but water descending at a dam will produce power. One law makes both happen. Gravity can help us or hurt us.

The laws of the spirit also work for us or against us. Wisdom is using them for powerful results. Foolishness is thinking that ignoring them will have no negative effects for us. Just as life's natural laws show "no partiality," neither are the laws of the spirit realm. Yes, we now have a covenant of blessing through believing, but our choices are still important. "Whatever a man sows, that will he also reap" (Galatians 6:7). Hosea said, "My people are destroyed for lack of knowledge" (Hosea 4:6). Truly, there is pain and difficulty when we don't have the wisdom of God's laws guiding our lives.

God has not predestined us to hardship, but has enabled us to release beneficial power through spiritual laws such as unity, forgiveness, giving first fruits to God, speaking life, and walking in thanksgiving. "Wisdom cries out... 'Whoever is simple, let him turn in here!'" (Proverbs 9:3, 4). Wisdom is this: understanding and walking in the laws of the spirit.

Declare

Like Solomon in 2 Chronicles 1, I cry out for the spirit of wisdom.
I am receiving revelation concerning the laws of the Spirit
that dramatically influence my life.
I release power all around me as I allow these laws to work for me.

26 VALUING JOY

A merry heart does good like a medicine.
Proverbs 17:22

*T*ake three times a day for ten days and you will get better. When a doctor gives these instructions, most people are going to obey. Why? They simply believe that it will work.

Our Great Physician has given us a prescription for health and strength. It is walking in joy. Dr. God says, "A merry heart does good like medicine" (Proverbs 17:22) and "the joy of the Lord is your strength" (Nehemiah 8:10). Indeed the Bible teaches that joy is essential to a victorious life.

A main aspect of joy is laughter. Studies have proven the benefits of laughter. Cancer patients have been healed through a prescription of watching funny movies. Cells that destroy tumors and viruses increase through hearty laughter. Energy-causing endorphins are released into our body's system through hilarity.

Samson had a secret to his strength (Judges 13-16). The Philistines sought to discover this mystery. Like Samson, we too have been given a secret for strength: It's joy. Let's not forget it. It is the wise person who finds ways to increase the powerful prescriptions of joy and laughter.

Declare

I thank You, Father, that You are now giving me the keys
to increase the "good medicine" in my life.
By Your Holy Spirit I will purpose to take this powerful prescription
every day so I can walk in health and strength
for the great days of harvest ahead. Amen.

WHAT ABOUT JOB?

What I feared has happened to me.
Job 3:25

*2**7***

*D*oes Job's experience (read Job 1 & 2) teach us that God will send death, sickness, lack, and devastation into our lives to test our love for Him? Does He "allow it" and let the devil be His instrument of trials and testing? Or is there another answer to this question about Christian suffering? Our answer will greatly affect the level of victory that we have in life.

Here's what this writer believes. Job said, "For the thing I greatly feared has come upon me" (Job 3:25). His fear gave Satan a legal access to "kill, steal, and destroy" from him. God "allowed" this attack only in the sense that He established spiritual laws (like the law of fear and the law of faith) that bring a result into our lives. Job's situation is similar to when Jesus told Peter, "Satan has asked for you, that he may sift you as wheat..." (Luke 22:31). Satan's eventual sifting of Peter resulted from a door of pride that Peter had opened. It was not a random attack, but manifested because of a violation of a spiritual law.

But, you might say, "We cannot take out the mystery of God. His ways are beyond human understanding." In response to this, I ask, "What then about God's promises? Are there any specific promises that we can truly believe (beyond eternal life and that "all things work together for good")? Are His promises always secondary to His sovereignty?" If we believe that, then it will be difficult to pray in faith again.

Declare

I live under a supernatural protection.
I am shutting doors in my life to the enemy.
I am opening doors for the blessing and power of God
to flow in me and through me.

WHAT ABOUT JOB?

All that he (Job) has is in your (Satan's) power.
Job 1:12

A traditional view concerning Job is this: God allowed Satan to ravage his life as a test of Job's character and love for God. This may sound plausible to some, but it is a teaching that leads to hopelessness and confusion about when we are to resist the devil.

We've already introduced Job 3:25 as the open door for Job's troubles - "For the thing I greatly feared has come on me." This fear is manifested in Job 1:4,5 where a worried and stressed out Job is continually offering sacrifices for his children. He was afraid that something bad was going to happen to them.

Look at verse twelve of chapter one. Notice what God said to Satan, "Behold, all that he has is in your power." This was not a handing over of Job to Satan, but a declaration of what was already true because of Job's open door of fear. God did not put Job in Satan's hands. Job's fear put him in the hands of the enemy.

Is this difficult to accept? Maybe, but the alternative view is even more implausible – saying that God will use the devil to kill our family, destroy our property, and afflict our body. Again, if we accept this second view, then we are destined to never be able to pray in faith for specific areas of our lives, nor can we ever really be confident of God's will in our lives.

Declare

God is good and Satan is bad.
Jesus came to destroy the works of the devil, not partner with him
to accomplish God's purposes.

Note: Even though fear is something to be uprooted in our lives, we thank God for His mercy and grace to protect us as we are on the journey of moving from fear to faith.

WHAT ABOUT JOB?

The Lord gave and the Lord has taken away.
Job 1:21

29

*W*hat are we to infer from the above statement by Job? Does this mean that God can, and sometimes will, "take away" our family, our health, our finances, and our possessions as part of His plan for our lives?

We know God inspired all of scripture, but not all passages or quotes in the Bible are God's thoughts. For instance, the book of Ecclesiastes was written by a backslidden Solomon. God inspired this entire book to be in the Bible, but we cannot accept every conclusion from Solomon in Ecclesiastes as God's thoughts; this writing is primarily an illustration of the cynicism and purposelessness that results from rejecting God.

Job's attitude of loving and blessing God during the toughest of times is powerful and is an example for us. We should not however allow Job's experience and conclusions to create our beliefs concerning the reason for negative things in life. If we accept a theology that the Lord gives and the Lord takes away in the areas of our health, protection, and loved ones; then there can be little faith in prayer. This would not be consistent with the message of the New Covenant.

Declare

Jesus has come to give me a more abundant life.
The enemy is a thief seeking to steal, kill, and destroy (John 10:10).
I resist him in Jesus' name.

30 JUDGING THE FAITH OF OTHERS
Faith working through love.
Galatians 5:6

*I*t is wise to use great caution when analyzing the faith of others. Here are three reasons why:

We don't know how far they've come - We all start at different places. Some have inherited a place of great blessing by the faith of others. Others have practically started at "square one" in their faith walk. In God's eyes, someone could have "great faith," but seem weaker than many others. "Man looks at the outward appearance, but the Lord looks at the heart" (I Samuel 16:7).

Corporate faith is more important than personal faith - Yes, individuals must take personal responsibility for their lives, but the local and regional church needs to be primarily concerned with possessing the "edifying of the body of Christ" (Ephesians 4:12), which will increase the level of blessing and protection in its area of influence.

Criticism and condemnation will actually decrease personal and corporate faith - Galatians 5:6 calls us to have "faith working through love." We need to look for ways to love and encourage people where they are at instead of being negative against seeming unbelief. Many people have become self-appointed faith police officers and have unwittingly caused hurt to others. Let's not be one of them.

Declare

The spirit of criticism is far from me.
I am an encourager of the faith of others.
I have great wisdom to know what to say, and what not to say,
to those who are in a faith battle.

FAITH AND MEDICINE

You will sustain him on his sick bed.
Psalms 41:3

We have a big covenant with God (Hebrews 8:6). This agreement with Him includes wonderful provision and promise for abundant health. Physical vitality is a major part of our benefit package (Psalms 103:2,3). Our faith needs to press in and receive what Jesus took stripes for (Isaiah 53:3-4).

With this in mind, should a person of faith take any medication? Is it permissible to consult doctors? Can we trust God to work through the medical profession or is this evidence of unbelief and putting our faith in man?

There are two extremes to avoid in this. The first is the reliance on man instead of God. Asa did this and was condemned (see 2 Chronicles 16:12). The other extreme is ignoring the fact that medicine ("use a little wine for your stomach's sake" - I Timothy 5:23) and doctors (for example Luke) are present in Scripture.

So what should we do? As an overcoming Christian, we should keep seeking to daily strengthen our faith. Like Abraham, we believe that next month and next year we will be able to receive more of God's promises in our lives. In the meantime, it can be wisdom (as part of our plan to strengthen our faith) to take medications and to benefit from the expertise of doctors. They will help us deal with symptoms in our physical bodies, as we keep pursuing being "fully convinced" (Romans 4:21) about our provision of abundant health for our lives.

Declare

I have wisdom concerning the use of medications and doctors.
I understand that God does miraculous healing
and also heals through doctors.

32

WRESTLING FOR WHAT?

I will not let you go.
Genesis 32:26

*J*acob wrestled with the angel and made a tenacious declaration, "I will not let You go unless You bless me." This bulldog boldness got God's attention.

How would God choose to bless this person who would not take no for an answer? Money? A long life? A new camel? Victory over his enemies? A resolving of a difficult matter? No, his blessing was a revelation of his real name, his true identity. His name would no longer be Jacob, but it would be Israel (Prince With God). His blessing was this: he would receive a new sense of who he really was, which would produce a change in his thoughts and vocabulary about himself. This, in turn, would cause a change in his actions and destiny.

The implications of this are revolutionary! One of the greatest things we can get from God is a revelation of who we really are. Once we call ourselves what God calls us, we will accelerate down the road of transformation.

We must move past just wanting God to fix our problems or to just have His blessing and anointing. We must get a hold of Him in our spirit and say, "I am not going to let You go unless You bless me with a true understanding of who I really am in You." Once this happens, everything changes.

Declare

I am a seeker of God. I go beyond simply wanting a situation changed.
I tenaciously seek Him and receive
His blessing of transformed-thoughts about my identity in Him.

Stop thinking of Christianity as a suppression of desire.
We do not repress. We pursue a new identity by faith.

*H*ere is a powerful truth for the victorious Christian: What we believe after we pray is just as important as what we believe when we pray. This principle is also true in ministry (what we believe after we minister is just as important as what we believe when we minister).

It is important to not withdraw faith after prayer or ministry. The devil wants us to curse the good seeds that have been sown by tempting us to speak unbelief concerning what has just been done. Certainly we can find areas where we can improve, but we must avoid negative, conclusions that can undo much of the good that happened.

Jesus cursed the fig tree in Mark 11. The next morning "they saw the fig tree dried up from the roots." This tells us two things. First, our influence in prayer and ministry starts in the unseen (in the roots); thus, outward results (whether circumstances or feelings) should not be used to measure success or failure. Secondly, Jesus' words cursed the fig tree. We need to know that our words are powerful, and that they can bless or curse spiritual seeds and "trees" around us.

So what do we say after we pray or after we minister? The wise believer says, "I refuse to withdraw my faith. God did great things. His word will not return void" (Isaiah 55:11).

Declare

I radically thank God after I pray or minister.
I only speak and declare faith-filled words over my past prayer or ministry.
I maintain and speak my faith; thus, I see a greater harvest.

34

ARE WE THERE YET?

I press toward the goal.
Philippians 3:14

*A*re we there yet? Every parent has probably heard this question innumerable times. The usual answer is, "Not yet, but we are getting closer."

We know that we are legally "there" in possessing all of God's promises, but we also know that we are not experientially "there" in many areas of what is legally ours. This is an important distinction to understand.

The maturing person of faith can admit, "I am not there yet. I am still experiencing such things as lack, sickness, confusion, failure, unsaved children, marital problems, and other curses because my life and faith have not developed to the place they will." Any other attitude creates hopelessness because we would believe we are victims and have no power concerning our future.

So let's keep moving forward in our faith. We personally may not completely get "there" in experiencing God's promises, but we should advance as far as we can so that our descendents (both spiritual and physical) can start at a better place than we did.

Declare

I will increasingly experience what is already legally mine.
Lack is decreasing as my faith increases,
and my faith is growing daily.

Like the men of faith of old, we will not see all
the promises manifest in our lifetime,
but we will make a difference for those who come after us.

ESCAPING INTO GOD

In His presence is fullness of joy.
Psalms 16:11

35

Our God is a refuge. How wonderful it is to regularly go into the secret place of His presence! We are transformed as we spend time with Him through worship, prayer, anointed ministry, and/or seeking Him with others.

Romans 15:13 says, "Now may the God of hope fill you with all joy and peace in believing." Even though we can be strongly touched in a meeting, we need to be more concerned with this question: what happens in us when the meeting ends or the music stops?

We need to escape into God and not simply escape from ourselves. It's possible to use the things of God as a diversion from our own need for personal healing. We may hope that the Spirit will do something, but without changing what we believe, it will only be short term. We cannot have a change in behavior without a change in the way we think.

What's the solution? Do we stop spending time in His presence? Of course not, but we need to expect a growing hope for our lives as a fruit of our times with Him. God's Spirit will loosen our spiritual soil so that the roots of hopelessness and unworthiness can be pulled out. Then we are truly escaping into God.

Declare

I love God's presence.
He is my refuge and strength.
Personal hope and joy are powerful fruits that come
from my "hiding place" times with God.

36 BECOMING FULLY CONVINCED

And being fully convinced...
Romans 4:21

*A*braham is the Bible's example of how to walk by faith. Even though he lived under the Old Covenant, he had a New Covenant revelation in regard to receiving from God. The victorious Christian must know what Abraham knew.

The Bible refers to different levels of faith. Jesus spoke of no faith, little faith, much faith, and great faith. Romans chapter four says that Abraham was "strengthened in faith" (vs. 20) and became "fully convinced that what He had promised, He was also able to perform" (vs. 21). Just as a weight lifter strengthens his muscles by pressing against resistance, the Christian can strengthen his faith through declaring God's Word and standing against negative looking circumstances. We can all move from no faith to the great faith of being fully convinced concerning God's promises.

Being "fully convinced" is our goal. It is important to know where we are going. As with Abraham, we must embrace the process that leads to this full assurance. God's promises are not automatically possessed simply because we are a Christian. They are received by a "convinced" faith.

Declare

Like Abraham did, I am moving forward in my faith
I am strengthened today as I declare truth even in the face
of seemingly dead circumstances.
I am becoming fully convinced.

CAUSE OF DISASTERS

I will heal their land.
2 Chronicles 7:14

*H*urricanes, floods, earthquakes, droughts, tornadoes, tsunamis, and other disasters happen around the earth. Are these random happenings that can occur anywhere and at any time? Are they God's judgments? Can we do anything to prevent them?

A disaster is an event that causes serious loss, destruction, hardship, unhappiness, or death. They did not exist on earth until Adam's rebellion, which set in motion earth's fury through natural disasters. There are no disasters in heaven right now. They are a curse and not a blessing.

Scripture shows that calamities have spiritual "roots." In 2 Samuel 21, Israel was experiencing a prolonged drought. King David sought God and discovered the reason was his predecessor's mistreatment of a certain people group. He corrected the problem and the drought ended. This passage and many others clearly show that blessing and protection are influenced greatly by sin, righteousness, faith, and fear.

Are disasters then judgments by an angry God? Has He finally "had enough" and then punishes people? No. A better understanding comes through this thought: protection has been removed through continual violation of spiritual laws. God did not choose judgment, but we chose to live life apart from where He and His protection are. Remember, God's spiritual laws will work for us or against us.

God's heart is not judgment (see Jonah), but He has allowed us to make our own choices that will influence the presence or absence of "natural" disasters.

Declare

Thank You God that we are humbling ourselves, standing in the righteousness You have given us, and praying.
Thank You that You have forgiven our sin and are healing our land.

38

ECONOMY, CLIMATE & HEALTH

If my people...
2 Chronicles 7:14

*C*an believers positively affect climatic weather patterns, the economy, and the physical health of a nation? One well-known Bible verse gives us a clue. "If My people who are called by My name will humble themselves, and pray and seek My face, and turn from their wicked ways, then I will hear from heaven, and will forgive their sin and heal their land" (2 Chronicles 7:14).

What does this healing consist of? If we look at verse thirteen of the same chapter, we see three areas of life to be "healed." God said, "When I shut up heaven and there is no rain (weather problems), or command the locusts to devour the land (economic difficulties) or send pestilence (plagues and health problems)..." After he listed these three problems, He says, "If My people..."

These negative circumstances are "sent by God" only in the sense that He has set up spiritual laws that, if honored, will bring blessing (and, if ignored, will bring difficulties). He does not "choose" for these to happen, but people do by ignoring His principles. The amazing thing to understand though is that God's people have the ability to impact three vital areas of life: climate, economy, and health. Yes, our belief in Jesus' death and resurrection is the key to spiritual transformation, but let's also press into the depths of 2 Chronicles 7:14 and help establish God's protection in every area where we have influence.

Declare

I am humbling myself, praying, seeking God's face
and embracing God's ways.
I am powerfully impacting my future and my nation's future.

ATTRACTING FAVOR OR REJECTION

As he thinks in his heart, so is he.
Proverbs 23:7

39

o our beliefs make a difference in how others treat us? Are strife and rejection simply bad luck while favor and acceptance are good luck? The Bible indicates that there are spiritual laws that influence these matters. As we have said, wisdom teaches us to make these laws work for us and for the kingdom of God.

Luke 6:37-38 states the law of reciprocity. "Judge not, and you shall not be judged. Condemn not, and you shall not be condemned. Forgive, and you will be forgiven. Give, and it will be given to you... For with the same measure that you use, it will be measured back to you." Our inner attitudes and our outward actions cause a "giving" that brings an experience back to us (in proportion to the amount we have given).

We love others to the degree we love ourselves, thus our attitude toward ourselves becomes the basis for attitudes we give to other people. This, in turn, releases a harvest (an experience) in accordance with the measure that has been given.

Complicated? No. As a man "thinks in his heart, so is he" (Proverbs 23:7). If a man thinks he is rejected, he is rejected. If a man thinks he is favored, he is favored. The key is to think about ourselves as God thinks about us.

Declare

God is good to me.
I expect and receive His goodness.
I give goodness to others in actions and attitudes.
I therefore increasingly receive goodness
and favor back in my relationships.

ATTRACTING FAVOR OR REJECTION

As he thinks in his heart, so is he.
Proverbs 23:7

Our beliefs make the difference in how others treat us. Indeed, strife and rejection are not simply bad luck, nor is favor and acceptance the result from good luck.

The Apostle Paul rebuked the Galatians by correcting a major doctrinal heresy that was blocking grace from their lives. They had moved from faith based Christianity to a performance based religion. One result of this emphasis on law was the biting and devouring of one another (Galatians 5:15). Their wrong beliefs about who they were in God actually attracted rejection and strife. They were cut off from grace (5:4), which blocked favor in relationships.

Those who have a "works doctrine" see themselves as rejected by God. This creates a performance environment where rejection and strife flourish. If we don't believe we have favor with God, how can we believe we could have favor with others? An unconscious thinking pattern will develop that believes mistreatment is deserved; thus, strife and rejection (biting and devouring) result.

On the contrary, those who believe they are radically favored (through Jesus) will have a positive expectancy of seeing His goodness in all aspects of life – including relationships. This belief will profoundly impact the increase of future "favor with God and man" (see Luke 2:52).

Declare

*God supplies His Spirit and works miracles among us
by the hearing of faith and not by the works of the law (Galatians 3:5).
I believe the report of God's favor over my life.
As Jesus did, I increase greatly in favor with both God and man.*

declaration list...one

A note on these declarations: We won't have something just because we say something, but saying something is necessary to having it. If at the beginning of the 40 days, you don't understand fully why these three sets of declarations are important, then speak them by faith anyway. Some of the first devotionals will give clarity as to their importance.

The following ten basic declarations are foundational to the building of your faith. They will increase expectancy of God's goodness, and will thus increase the manifestation of that goodness in your life. Say these (and the other declarations' lists) every day for a month and see what happens to your life. Romans 4:17; Romans 10:9,10

1. My prayers are powerful and effective.
   2 Corinthians 5:21; James 5:16b

2. God richly supplies all my needs. **Philippians 4:19**

3. I am dead to sin and have a victorious DNA in me.
   Romans 6:11; Romans 5:17

4. I walk in ever increasing health.
   Isaiah 53:3-5; Psalm 103:1-5

5. I live under a supernatural protection.
   Psalm 91; Hebrews 8:6

6. I prosper in all my relationships. **Luke 2:52**

7. I consistently bring God encounters to other people.
   Mark 16:17,18; Acts 3:6

8. In Jesus, I am 100% loved and worthy to experience all of God's blessings. **Colossians 1:12-15**

9. Each of my family members is wonderfully blessed and radically loves Jesus. **Acts 16:30, 31**

10. I uproariously laugh when I hear a lie from the devil.
    Psalm 2:2-4

declaration list . . two

Remember this: Faith is the evidence of things not seen (Hebrews 11:1). God's promises, not our circumstances, are our *evidence* for what is really true. We don't deny negative facts in our lives, but we choose to focus on the higher reality of God's truth. Faith indeed comes by hearing (Romans 10:17); therefore, we choose to speak these powerful truths to build our own faith (believing Romans 12:2 – that our experience will catch up to our beliefs).

1. I set the course of my life with my words.
    James 3:2-5; Proverbs 18:21

2. God is on my side; therefore, I declare that I cannot be defeated.
    Romans 8:37; Psalm 91; Philippians 4:13

3. I am the head, not the tail. I have insight. I have wisdom. I have ideas and divine strategies. I have authority.
    Deuteronomy 8:18; 28:13; James 1:5-8; Luke 10:19

4. My family and those connected to us are protected from disasters, disease, divorce, adultery, poverty, false accusation, foolish decisions and all accidents.   **Psalm 91**

5. As Abraham did, I speak God's promises over my life so that my faith is strengthened to possess all of God's promises.
    Romans 4:17-23

6. I have a sound mind. I think the right thoughts, say the right words, and make the right decisions in every situation I face.
    2 Timothy 1:7

7. I expect to have powerful, divine appointments today to heal the sick, raise the dead, prophesy life, lead people to Christ, bring deliverance, release signs and wonders, and bless every place I go.
    The book of Acts

8. I expect that today will be the best day of my life spiritually, emotionally, relationally, and financially in Jesus' name.
    Romans 15:13

declaration list... three

One of the main *methods* Jesus and the apostles used (in the Gospels and Acts) was to SPEAK TO things. You will notice that they did not ask God to heal people, cast out demons, or raise the dead; *but they spoke to bodies, demons, the wind, etc. And* Jesus, in Mark 11:23, also encourages us to speak to mountains that are in our life.

This set of declarations specifically focuses on our speaking to the various aspects in our lives.

1. My angels are carrying out the Word of God on my behalf.
   Psalm 103:2

2. All attacks that were headed my way are diverted right now through angelic protection in Jesus' name.
   Psalm 91

3. Just as Jesus spoke to the wind, I say, "Peace be still to my mind, emotions, body and family."
   Mark 4:39

4. I speak to every mountain of discouragement, stress, depression and lack, and say, "Be cast into the sea in Jesus' name."
   Mark 11:22-24

5. I say to this day, "You are blessed!" And I declare that I serve a mighty God, who today will do exceedingly and abundantly beyond all that I can ask or think. I say you are a good God, and I eagerly anticipate your goodness today.
   Ephesians 3:20

suggested bible reading plan

Day 1: Hebrews 4

Day 2: Romans 4

Day 3: Galatians 1

Day 4: Galatians 2

Day 5: Galatians 3

Day 6: Galatians 4

Day 7: Galatians 5

Day 8: Galatians 6

Day 9: Philippians 1

Day 10: Philippians 2

Day 11: Philippians 3

Day 12: Philippians 4

Day 13: Mark 1

Day 14: Mark 2

Day 15: Mark 3

Day 16: Mark 4

Day 17: Mark 5

Day 18: Mark 6

Day 19: Mark 7

Day 20: Mark 8

Day 21: Mark 9

Day 22: Mark 10

Day 23: Mark 11

Day 24: Proverbs 1

Day 25: Proverbs 3

Day 26: Proverbs 4

Day 27: Proverbs 8

Day 28: Proverbs 10

Day 29: Proverbs 14

Day 30: Proverbs 15

Day 31: Proverbs 18

Day 32: Romans 4

Day 33: Galatians 3

Day 34: Galatians 4

Day 35: Galatians 5

Day 36: Galatians 6

Day 37: Philippians 1

Day 38: Philippians 2

Day 39: Philippians 3

Day 40: Philippians 4

Some chapters are recommended more than once.

about the authors

The Backlunds were senior pastors for seventeen years before joining the team at Bethel Church (Redding, California) in 2008. Ten of those years were spent on the backside of the desert in Central Nevada where they led  their church into renewal and significant growth.

In 2001 Bill Johnson and Kris Vallotton called Steve and Wendy to be senior leaders at Mountain Chapel in Weaverville, California (the church that Bill pastored for seventeen years). As a result of these experiences, Steve and Wendy developed a special heart for senior leaders and other church leaders which led them to their current position at Bethel Church which focuses on leader development in *Bethel School of Supernatural Ministry* and through online curriculum for leaders around the world.

Their website, www.ignitedhope.com and their ministry through Bethel Church (www.igloballegacy.org), are dedicated to the health and strength of leaders around the world.

Victorious Mindsets

What we believe is ultimately more important than what we do. The course of our lives is set by our deepest core beliefs. Our mindsets are either a stronghold for God's purposes or a playhouse for the enemy. In this book, fifty biblical attitudes are revealed that are foundational for those who desire to walk in freedom and power.

Cracks in the Foundation

Going to a higher level in establishing key beliefs will affect ones intimacy with God and fruitfulness for the days ahead. This book challenges many basic assumptions of familiar Bible verses and common Christian phrases that block numerous benefits of our salvation. The truths shared in this book will help fill and repair "cracks" in our thinking which rob us of our God-given potential.

You're Crazy If You Don't Talk to Yourself

Jesus did not just think His way out of the wilderness and neither can we. He spoke truth to invisible beings and mindsets that sought to restrict and defeat Him. This book reveals that life and death are truly in the power of the tongue and emphasize the necessity of speaking truth to our souls. Our words really do set the course of our lives and the lives of others. (Proverbs 18:21)

Let's Just Laugh at That

Our hope level is an indicator of whether we are believing truth or lies. Truth creates hope and freedom, but believing lies brings hopelessness and restriction. We can have great theology but still be powerless because of deception about the key issues of life. Many of these self-defeating mindsets exist in our subconscious and have never been identified. This book exposes numerous falsehoods and reveals truth that makes us free. Get ready for a joy-infused adventure into hope-filled living.

additional resources

Divine Strategies for Increase

The laws of the spirit are more real than the natural laws. God's laws are primarily principles to release blessing, not rules to be obeyed to gain right standing with God. The Psalmist talks of one whose greatest delight is in the law of the Lord. This delight allows one to discover new aspects of the nature of God (hidden in each law) to behold and worship. The end result of this delighting is a transformed life that prospers in every endeavor. His experience can be our experience, and this book unlocks the blessings hidden in the spiritual realm.

Possessing Joy

In His presence is fullness of joy (Psalm 16:11). Joy is to increase as we go deeper in our relationship with God. Religious tradition has devalued the role that gladness and laughter have for personal victory and kingdom advancement. His presence may not always produce joy; but if we never or rarely have fullness of joy, we must reevaluate our concept of God. This book takes one on a journey toward the headwaters of the full joy that Jesus often spoke of. Get ready for joy to increase and strength and longevity to ignite.

Higher Perspectives

The Bible introduces us to people who saw life's circumstances from a heavenly perspective. They were not "realistic," but supernatural in their viewpoint. As a result, they became history makers. Their experience is an invitation for us to live and see as they did. This book reveals fifty scriptural higher perspectives that will jolt you out of low-level thinking and increase your capacity to experience all of the promises of God in your life.

Audio message series are available through the Igniting Hope store at: www.ignitedhope.com.

Printed in Great Britain
by Amazon